PIKACHU CROCHET KIT

EVERYTHING YOU NEED TO MAKE PIKACHU AND INSTRUCTIONS FOR 5 OTHER POKÉMON

Sabrina Somers

DAVID & CHARLES
—PUBLISHING—

www.davidandcharles.com

Publishing Director: Ame Verso
Head of Design: Anna Wade
Designer: Insight Design Concepts Ltd
Technical Editor: Carol Ibbetson
Photography: The Really Good Media Company
Packager: BlueRed Press Ltd

David and Charles publishes high-quality books on a wide range of
subjects. For more information visit
www.davidandcharles.com.

This book is part of the Pikachu Crochet Kit and is not to be sold
separately.

Figures on cover not to scale.

INTRODUCTION

SKILL LEVELS

All Pokémon players need to train—themselves and their Pokémon. The same is true with crochet. To help in your training, the projects start with easy techniques. Later, they get a bit more difficult. For this kit I have designed six Pokémon for you to make. Which one will be your favorite?

A few words of advice—don't rush to do a difficult one until you have mastered the basics of crochet and construction. Start with an easy character, then go for it!

My Pokémon are presented in three levels of difficulty, each designated by a yellow line, the longer the line, the more difficult the crochet.

BEGINNER

The easiest are Jigglypuff and Snorlax

EASY

The next group are Eevee, Pikachu, and Psyduck.

INTERMEDIATE

Finally, the hardest Pokémon is Vulpix.

It doesn't matter whether you're a beginner or an expert, all of the patterns produce wonderful Pokémon! Keep them yourself—or give them as gifts.

I had great fun creating these patterns and I really hope that you enjoy making them too.

DIFFICULTY LEVELS
BEGINNER
EASY
INTERMEDIATE

WINDING A SKEIN INTO A BALL
STEP 1

To avoid your yarn tangling, it's highly recommended that you wind it into a ball before you begin. Winding yarn into a ball by hand is very simple. Unfold the skein so it forms one big loop. Begin by finding an end, wrap the yarn around three fingers a few dozen times. Carefully slide the yarn off your fingers keeping it neatly contained.

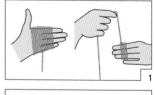

STEP 2

Fold the yarn in half over itself and continue to wind the string tightly around the tiny ball. It may look a little messy in the beginning, but as you continue to wind and turn the ball of yarn, it starts to take shape beautifully.

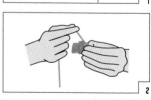

STEP 3

As you wind the yarn, be sure to twist the ball around to evenly distribute the yarn. Continue in this way until you have a ball!

TOOLS AND MATERIALS

CROCHET HOOK

There are numerous sizes of crochet hooks available, made of metal or plastic, and in several different lengths. You can simply change the size of your Pokémon by using a thicker or a smaller hook.

NOTE: It's very important to combine the thickness of the yarn with the correctly sized hook. On the label around the yarn you can find the recommended hook size. To create tight crochet work without big gaps—I recommend using a slightly smaller hook than indicated on the label.

TEXTILE MARKERS

Some Pokémon have eyes that are too small to cut from felt. In these cases you can put a dot in with a black textile marker instead.

FELT

To create the face and other small details on your Pokémon you need different color felts. Use thin felt for the best results; thick felt can look out of scale and clumsy.

YARN NEEDLE

After crocheting you'll need a needle to sew all the parts together. A large sewing needle is ideal. Alternatively, use a darning needle or tapestry needle—whichever you prefer.

PINS

Although pins are not really necessary, they can be very useful when making your Pokémon. By pinning all the parts together before sewing, you can decide how your Pokémon will stand, and change its posture if needed. But remember to take all the pins out afterward!

GLUE

You will need glue to stick the felt details to your Pokémon. Use a fabric glue for the most successful results. Make sure you cover the entire area with only a thin layer of glue—a thick layer will be visible through the felt.

FIBERFILL STUFFING

Fill your Pokémon with synthetic fiberfill, which is usually made of fluffed out polyester. Stuff your character firmly, but be particularly careful not to overfill it, as the yarn will stretch and the filling will be visible through the holes in the stitches. This spoils the effect.

BRUSH

Used for fluffy parts—such as Eevee's collar—to fluff out the yarn. I recommend using a sharp brush with steel bristles. Failing that, a good hard bristle brush, or even an old toothbrush will do the trick.

SCISSORS

You will need scissors to cut off the yarn when you've finished and for cutting out the felt pieces. Some of the pieces are quite small and fiddly, so to get the best result with your felt, I heartily recommend small, sharp scissors.

STITCH MARKERS

Most parts of the Pokémon are made in continuous rounds—you can't see a clear beginning or end. So, to keep track of the rounds, I recommend the use of a stitch marker. Place it at the end of the round: after crocheting the next round, you should end up right above the stitch marker. Now move the stitch marker up to the end of the last round. This way you will keep track of your pattern.

COTTON YARN

In the patterns I have specified the type of yarn I used. Personally, I like to work with cotton yarn, because it makes the crochet work look tight and neat, but you can use any kind of yarn or wool you feel comfortable with. For the fluffy parts, like the flames, it's better to use acrylic yarn as it unravels easily and can look really effective.

TECHNIQUES

TERMINOLOGY

In the book we are using US crochet terms.

ABBREVIATIONS

US	UK
CH – chain	**CH** – chain
TCH – turning chain	**TCH** – turning chain
SL.ST – slipstitch	**SL.ST** – slipstitch
SC – single crochet	**DC** – double crochet
HDC – half double crochet	**HTR** – half treble crochet
DC – double crochet	**TR** – treble crochet
TC – triple crochet	**DTR** – double triple crochet
DEC – decrease	**DEC** – decrease
RND – round	**RND** – round
ROW – row	**ROW** – row

NB. It is very important to distinguish between rounds and rows. Rounds go round and round and continue to work in the same direction, while rows are worked from side to side, then back again.

HOW TO READ PATTERNS

The Pokémon are mainly made in continuous rounds of stitches. At the beginning of each line you will find "RND" with the number of the round. But for some pieces you need to work in rows, where you turn your work to crochet the next row back. In this case the number of the row is indicated with "ROW."

At the end of each line, a number in brackets will show you the number of stitches you should have at the end of this round/row.

When you find the line "2 sc in each 4th sc," for example, it means you need to crochet one stitch (1 sc) in the first, second, and third stitch, and two stitches (2 sc) in the fourth stitch (4th sc), and repeat this until the end of the round.

This works in the same way for decreasing. When you find the line "dec over each 4th and 5th sc," it means you need to crochet one stitch (1 sc) in the first, second, and third stitch, and decrease over the next two stitches (2 sc) and repeat this, until the end of the round.

You may also find a line like this: "2 sc in the 1st, 2nd, 3rd sc." In this case you need to crochet two stitches (2 sc) in the indicated stitches, and crochet one stitch (1 sc) in the remaining stitches of the round. The following instruction should be read as, repeat the instructions between the two asterisks 3 times in total.

2 ch + 1 tch, turn around and crochet 2 sl.st 3x.

You must never skip a stitch and always finish the complete round unless specifically told otherwise.

BASIC STITCHES EXPLAINED

MAGIC RING

The Pokémon are mainly made in rounds. To start a round you usually use a technique called the magic ring. Until you get used to it, this can be a little bit fiddly as the yarn wants to twist away from you: just hold the yarn gently, but firmly and it will work.

1. Create a loop with the yarn by wrapping it over two fingers, then use your hook to pull the long length side of the yarn through the loop. (Like a big, loose stitch).

2. Don't pull it tight, you need to keep the ring big enough for your hook to work in and out of easily.

3. Wrap the long side of the yarn over the hook and pull it through the loop on your hook.

You have now completed the base of the magic ring. Continue on:

4. Insert the hook into the ring.

5. Wrap the long side of the yarn over your hook and pull it through the ring. You should have two loops around the hook.

6. Wrap the long side of the yarn over your hook and pull it through the two loops.

You have now completed the first single crochet in the magic ring.

7. Repeat Steps 4 to 7 until you have made the indicated amount of single crochet stitches into the ring. For most patterns you need to make six single crochet stitches into the ring.

8. Now pull carefully on the short side of the yarn to close the ring. You now have a filled disk of stitches.

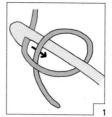

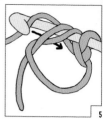

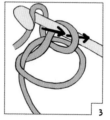

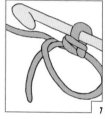

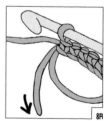

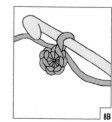

CHAIN (CH)

Chain stitch is used in most patterns and is the basis of most crochet. If you need to work in rows, your first (base) row will be a series of chain stitches.

1. Create a loop with the yarn and use your hook to pull the long side of the yarn through the loop.

2. Pull the end to tighten the knot.

3. Wrap the long side of the yarn over your hook and pull it through the loop on your hook.

4. You have completed the first chain stitch.

5. Repeat Step 3.

6. Continue until you've made the indicated number of chain stitches you need for the pattern. In my patterns I also use the term "turning chain" (tch), this is the same as a normal chain stitch, but you do this at the end of a row. After you turn around your work, you skip this first stitch and continue with the second chain stitch from your hook.

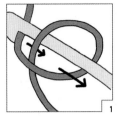

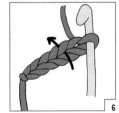

SINGLE CROCHET (SC)

My Pokémon are primarily made using the single crochet stitch. To start, first make a magic ring or chain before you make a single crochet.

1. Insert the hook into the next stitch.

2. Wrap your yarn over the hook and pull it through the stitch. Now you should have two loops on your hook.

3. Wrap the yarn over the hook and pull it through both loops.

4. You have completed a single crochet, now continue with the next one.

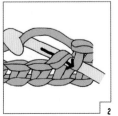
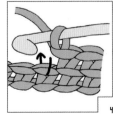

SLIP STITCH (SL.ST)

All Pokémon patterns contain the slip stitch. This stitch is mainly used to tie off your crochet piece.

1. Insert your hook into the next stitch.

2. Wrap the yarn over the hook.

3. Pull it through the stitch and the loop on your hook.

4. Completed slip stitch.

INCREASE (2 SC IN 1 STITCH)

To increase, you crochet two single crochet stitches into one stitch.

1. Make a single crochet.

2. Continue working into the same stitch and crochet another single crochet. Now you have an extra stitch in your round (or row).

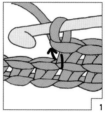
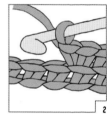

DECREASE WHILE CROCHETING IN ROUNDS (DEC)

This decreasing technique is only possible when you crochet in rounds.

1. Insert your hook into the front loop of the first stitch.

2. Insert your hook into the front loop of the second stitch.

3. Wrap the yarn over the hook and pull it through the two front loops. You should have two loops on your hook.

4. Wrap the yarn over the hook and pull it through the remaining loops. Now you have one stitch less in your round.

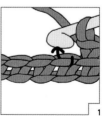
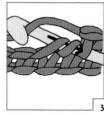
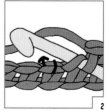
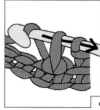

DECREASE WHILE CROCHETING IN ROWS OR BACK LOOPS (DEC)

When you crochet in rows, or when you need to crochet in the back loops only, you can't use the previous technique. Instead:

1. Insert your hook into the first stitch.

2. Wrap the yarn over the hook and pull it through the stitch. Now insert your hook in the second stitch, wrap the yarn over the hook and pull it through this stitch too. You should now have three loops on your hook.

3. Wrap the yarn over the hook and pull it through the three loops. Now you have one stitch less in your row.

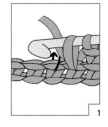

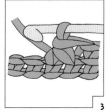

DOUBLE CROCHET (DC)

A double crochet is bigger than a single crochet. To start a double crochet you often need to crochet a few chain stitches to gain height, but it's not always necessary.

1. Wrap the yarn over your hook and insert the hook through the next stitch.

2. Wrap the yarn over your hook and pull it through the stitch. You should now have three loops on your hook.

3. Wrap the yarn over the hook and pull it through the first two loops on your hook. You should have two loops remaining on your hook.

4. Wrap the yarn over your hook and pull it through the remaining two loops.

5. You have completed the double crochet.

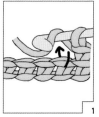
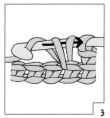
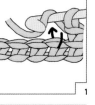

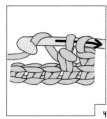
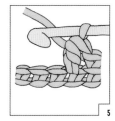

HALF DOUBLE CROCHET (HDC)

The half double crochet is slightly smaller than a double crochet.

1. Wrap the yarn over the hook and insert it into the next stitch.

2. Wrap the yarn over the hook and pull it through the stitch. You should have three loops on your hook.

3. Wrap the yarn over the hook and pull it through all three loops on the hook.

4. You have completed the half double crochet.

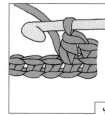

CROCHET IN THE FRONT OR BACK LOOPS

Normally when you make a single crochet you go through the whole stitch—which means you go through both loops. Sometimes the pattern instructs you to crochet in the front (1) or back (2) loops only. This can be necessary to create an edge, for example.

SPECIAL TECHNIQUES

BIND OFF

You usually bind off (fasten off) with a slip stitch. For this, cut the remaining yarn, but leave a tail, usually enough to sew in later.

1. Crochet a slip stitch.

2. Pull on the loop until the entire yarn length is through it.

3. When you crochet in rows it is not always possible to bind off with a slip stitch. In this case you fasten off with an extra chain stitch.

4. Pull the cut yarn fully through the stitch.

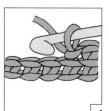
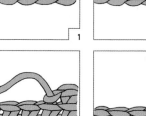
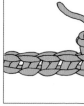

COLOR SWITCH

To switch colors you start one stitch before it's indicated in the pattern, but it will only become visible from the next stitch.

1. Insert the hook into the next stitch.

2. Wrap the old color over your hook and pull it through the stitch.

3. You should have two loops on your hook.

4. Wrap the new color over your hook and pull it through both loops.

5. Cut the old color and tie the end to the short side of the new color on the inside of your work.

6. Continue with the new color.

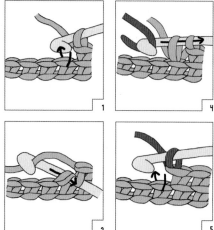

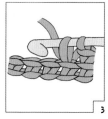

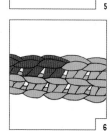

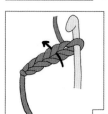

STARTING A ROUND WITH A CHAIN

To create an oval piece you sometimes need to start with a chain instead of a magic ring.

1. Begin with as many chain stitches as instructed.

2. Turn around and crochet a single crochet in each chain stitch (unless told otherwise), don't forget to skip the turning chain.

3. Turn your work upside down to crochet into the other side of the chain stitches.

4. Crochet a single crochet in each chain stitch (unless told otherwise). Don't turn the work round, but continue working in spirals.

MAKING UP

CLOSING A PIECE

When you make a piece that needs to be closed at the end, you often end with six single crochet stitches. This leaves a small gap in your work.

1. To close a gap, crochet a slip stitch and cut the yarn, but leave sufficient tail to sew in later.

2. Attach the remaining yarn to a needle and go through the front loop of the first stitch.

3. Then go through the front loop of the next stitch.

4. Continue until you complete the round. Pull the yarn tight to minimize the gap.

5. Go through the center of the gap and finish on the other side of the piece.

6. Pull it tight and cut the remaining yarn.

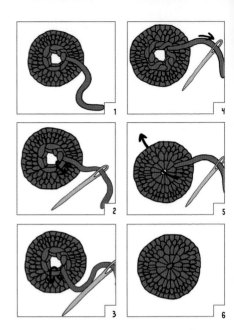

CROCHETING TWO PARTS TOGETHER

Sometimes you need to crochet multiple parts together. In the patterns, for example, the instruction is "crochet sc around the two parts."

1. Place the crochet pieces next to each other. Instead of crocheting in the next stitch of the current piece (b), insert your hook in a stitch of piece (a).

2. Crochet a single crochet and continue with that piece. When you've completed the round in piece (a), continue with the round you started with, ie. piece (b). Complete that round too. Sometimes it is necessary to skip a few stitches of a piece or to crochet the parts in a specific order. In this case it will be indicated in the pattern.

EMBROIDERY

Most of the Pokémon need some embroidery—to create a mouth for example.

1. Attach the yarn to a needle and go through a random stitch. Bring the yarn out where you want the mouth to begin.

2. Then go through the stitch where you want the mouth to end.

3. Bring the yarn out at the same stitch as the other yarn end—so where you started.

4. Tie the two yarn ends together and tuck the remaining yarn inside your piece.

If you need to make a curve, you can carefully put fabric glue between the yarn and your piece to create a shape.

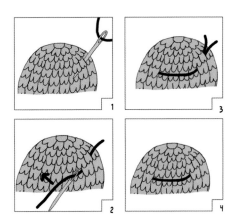

SEWING TWO PIECES TOGETHER

After you've made all the pieces for a character, you can start sewing them together. To decide the exact location for each part I recommend fixing all the pieces with pins first. To make this clear, I've made the pieces blue and red.

1. Thread the tail of the red piece through a needle. Take it through the first stitch of the blue piece where the red piece needs to be attached.

2. Push the needle from back to front through the next stitch of the red piece.

3. Go through the blue piece where you ended at Step 1 and come out on the other side of the next stitch.

4. Pull it tight. Repeat Steps 2 and 3 for all the stitches of the red piece.

After sewing the pieces together, go through the blue piece again, and let the yarn come out at a random place far from the red part. Cut the remaining yarn.

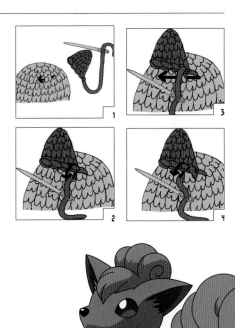

JIGGLYPUFF

OFFICIAL COLORS

NATIONAL POKÉDEX NO.	TYPE	WEIGHT	HEIGHT
39	Normal - Fairy	12.1 lb / 5.5 kg	1ft 8 in / 0.5 m

If you have a busy day ahead, avoid looking deep into Jigglypuff's pretty, round eyes. You could end up so mesmerized, you won't even notice when it starts singing a lullaby to put you to sleep.

MATERIALS

- Crochet hook 2.5 mm

- 60 grams of pink yarn (I used Katia Capri—121)

- 5 grams of black yarn (I used Phildar Phil Coton 3—Noir 1200)

- Fiberfill

- White and teal felt

- Thin black yarn (for instance Rico Essentials Crochet—12)

Finished size approximately 4$\frac{1}{4}$ inches (11 cm) high

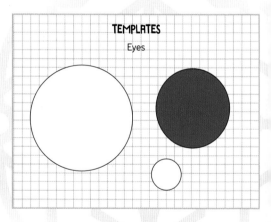

TEMPLATES

Eyes

HEAD/BODY

(Use pink yarn)

RND 1: 6 sc in magic ring (6)

RND 2: 2 sc in each sc (12)

RND 3: 2 sc in each 2nd sc (18)

RND 4: 2 sc in each 3rd sc (24)

RND 5: 2 sc in each 4th sc (30)

RND 6: 2 sc in each 5th sc (36)

RND 7: 2 sc in each 6th sc (42)

RND 8: 2 sc in each 7th sc (48)

RND 9: 2 sc in each 8th sc (54)

RND 10: 2 sc in each 9th sc (60)

RND 11: 60 sc (60)

RND 12: 2 sc in each 10th sc (66)

RND 13: 66 sc (66)

RND 14: 2 sc in each 11th sc (72)

RND 15–23: 72 sc (72)

RND 24: dec over each 11th and 12th sc (66)

RND 25: 66 sc (66)

RND 26: dec over each 10th and 11th sc (60)

RND 27: 60 sc (60)

RND 28: dec over each 9th and 10th sc (54)

RND 29: dec over each 8th and 9th sc (48)

RND 30: dec over each 7th and 8th sc (42)

RND 31: dec over each 6th and 7th sc (36)

RND 32: dec over each 5th and 6th sc (30)

RND 33: dec over each 4th and 5th sc (24)

Start filling and keep filling until the last round.

RND 34: dec over each 3rd and 4th sc (18)

RND 35: dec over each 2nd and 3rd sc (12)

RND 36: dec over each 2 sc (6)

Tie-off with a sl.st and close the head/body.

FEET (2x)

(Use pink yarn)

RND 1: 6 sc in magic ring (6)

RND 2: 2 sc in each 2nd sc (9)

RND 3: 9 sc (9)

RND 4: 2 sc in each 3rd sc (12)

RND 5: 12 sc (12)

RND 6: 2 sc in each 4th sc (15)

RND 7–8: 15 sc (15)

RND 9: dec over each 4th and 5th sc (12)

RND 10: 12 sc (12)

RND 11: dec over each 3rd and 4th sc (9)

RND 12: dec over each 2nd and 3rd sc (6)

Tie-off with a sl.st and close the feet. Let the yarn come out on the top of the feet and leave enough for sewing.

ARMS (2x)

(Use pink yarn)

RND 1: 6 sc in magic ring (6)

RND 2: 6 sc (6)

RND 3: 2 sc in each 2nd sc (9)

RND 4–5: 9 sc (9)

RND 6: 2 sc in each 3rd sc (12)

RND 7: 12 sc (12)

Fill the arms. Tie-off with a sl.st and leave enough yarn for sewing.

HEAD/BODY

FOOT

ARM

17

OUTER EARS (2x)

(Use pink yarn)

RND 1: 6 sc in magic ring (6)

RND 2: 6 sc (6)

RND 3: 2 sc in each sc (12)

RND 4: 12 sc (12)

RND 5: 2 sc in each 2nd sc (18)

RND 6: 18 sc (18)

RND 7: 2 sc in each 3rd sc (24)

RND 8: 24 sc (24)

RND 9: 2 sc in each 4th sc (30)

RND 10: 30 sc (30)

RND 11: 2 sc in each 5th sc (36)

Fill the ears slightly. Tie-off with a sl.st and leave enough yarn for sewing.

INNER EARS (2x)

(Use black yarn)

ROW 1: 1 ch + 1 tch (1)

ROW 2: turn around and crochet 2 sc in the ch + 1 tch (2)

ROW 3: turn around and crochet 2 sc in the 2nd sc + 1 tch (3)

ROW 4: turn around and crochet 2 sc in the 3rd sc + 1 tch (4)

ROW 5: turn around and crochet 2 sc in the 4th sc + 1 tch (5)

ROW 6: turn around and crochet 2 sc in the 5th sc + 1 tch (6)

ROW 7: turn around and crochet 2 sc in the 6th sc (7)

Tie-off and leave enough yarn for sewing.

CURL

(Use pink yarn)

RND 1: 6 sc in magic ring (6)

RND 2: 2 sc in each sc (12)

RND 3: 2 sc in each 2nd sc (18)

RND 4–6: 18 sc (18)

RND 7: dec over the 1st and 2nd, 3rd and 4th, 5th and 6th, 7th and 8th, 9th and 10th, 11th and 12th sc (12)

RND 8: 2 sc in each 2nd sc (18)

RND 9: 18 sc (18)

RND 10: 2 sc in each 3rd sc (24)

RND 11–16: 24 sc (24)

RND 17: dec over each 3rd and 4th sc (18)

Fill the curl slightly.

RND 18: 18 sc (18)

RND 19: dec over each 2nd and 3rd sc (12)

RND 20: dec over each 2 sc (6)

Tie-off with a sl.st and close the curl. Let the yarn come out on the top of the curl and leave enough for sewing.

Glue the protruding part of round 6 to round 10 to create a better curl shape.

OUTER EAR

INNER EAR

CURL

ASSEMBLY

Sew the feet to the bottom of the body.

Sew the arms to the body, at round 24 to round 27.

Sew the inner ears to the outer ears. Then sew the ears to the head, at round 5 to round 15.

Sew the curl to the head, at round 3 to round 13.

FACE

Cut two eyes out of white and teal felt. Glue these onto the head, at round 13 to round 20, with seven stitches between the eyes.

Embroider a mouth on the head using thin black yarn, at round 21.

SNORLAX

OFFICIAL COLORS

NATIONAL POKÉDEX NO.	TYPE	WEIGHT	HEIGHT
143	Normal	1014.1 lb/ 460.0 kg	6 ft 11 in / 2.1 m

If you find some expired food in your pantry, there's no need to throw it out! Snorlax will happily snarf it down—its stomach doesn't seem to mind.

MATERIALS

- Crochet hook 2.5 mm

- 60 grams of dark teal yarn (I used Scheepjes Catona—391)

- 15 grams of cream yarn (I used Scheepjes Catona—404)

- 5 grams of light blue yarn (I used Lana Grossa Cotone—78)

- Fiberfill

- White and brown felt

- Thin black yarn (I used Rico Essentials Crochet—12)

Finished size approximately 5$\frac{1}{2}$ inches (14 cm) high

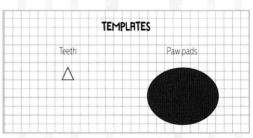

TEMPLATES

Teeth

Paw pads

HEAD/BODY

(Use dark teal yarn)

RND 1: 6 sc in magic ring (6)

RND 2: 2 sc in each sc (12)

RND 3: 2 sc in each 2nd sc (18)

RND 4: 2 sc in each 3rd sc (24)

RND 5: 2 sc in each 4th sc (30)

RND 6: 2 sc in each 5th sc (36)

RND 7: 2 sc in each 6th sc (42)

RND 8: 2 sc in each 14th sc (45)

RND 9–13: 45 sc (45)

RND 14: dec over each 14th and 15th sc (42)

RND 15: dec over each 5th and 6th sc (35)

RND 16: 2 sc in each 5th sc (42)

RND 17: 2 sc in each 7th sc (48)

RND 18: 2 sc in each 8th sc (54)

RND 19: 2 sc in each 9th sc (60)

RND 20: 60 sc (60)

RND 21: 2 sc in each 10th sc (66)

RND 22: 66 sc (66)

RND 23: 2 sc in each 11th sc (72)

RND 24–35: 72 sc (72)

RND 36: dec over each 11th and 12th sc (66)

RND 37: dec over each 10th and 11th sc (60)

RND 38: dec over each 9th and 10th sc (54)

RND 39: dec over each 8th and 9th sc (48)

RND 40: dec over each 7th and 8th sc (42)

RND 41: dec over each 6th and 7th sc (36)

Start filling and keep filling until the last round.

RND 42: dec over each 5th and 6th sc (30)

RND 43: dec over each 4th and 5th sc (24)

RND 44: dec over each 3rd and 4th sc (18)

RND 45: dec over each 2nd and 3rd sc (12)

RND 46: dec over each 2 sc (6)

Tie-off with a sl.st and close the body.

HEAD/BODY

BELLY/FACE

(Use cream yarn)

Note that you start at the bottom of the body and end with the top of the face.

ROW 1: 8 ch + 1 tch (8)

ROW 2: turn around and crochet 2 sc in the 1st, 8th ch + 1 tch (10)

ROW 3: turn around and crochet 2 sc in the 1st, 10th sc + 1 tch (12)

ROW 4: turn around and crochet 2 sc in the 1st, 12th sc + 1 tch (14)

ROW 5: turn around and crochet 2 sc in the 1st, 14th sc + 1 tch (16)

ROW 6: turn around and crochet 2 sc in the 1st, 16th sc + 1 tch (18)

ROW 7–16: turn around and crochet 18 sc + 1 tch (18)

ROW 17: turn around and dec over the 1st and 2nd, 17th and 18th sc + 1 tch (16)

ROW 18: turn around and dec over the 1st and 2nd, 15th and 16th sc + 1 tch (14)

ROW 19: turn around and dec over the 1st and 2nd, 13th and 14th sc + 1 tch (12)

ROW 20: turn around and dec over the 1st and 2nd, 11th and 12th sc + 1 tch (10)

ROW 21: turn around and dec over the 1st and 2nd, 9th and 10th sc + 1 tch (8)

ROW 22: turn around and crochet 2 sc in the 1st, 8th sc + 1 tch (10)

ROW 23: turn around and crochet 2 sc in the 1st, 10th sc + 1 tch (12)

ROW 24: turn around and crochet 2 sc in the 1st, 12th sc + 1 tch (14)

ROW 25–26: turn around and crochet 14 sc + 1 tch (14)

ROW 27: turn around and dec over the 1st and 2nd, 13th and 14th sc (12)

ROW 28: with the same side facing attach yarn to the centre of row 28 to work the other side and crochet 6 sc + 1 tch (6)

ROW 29: turn around and dec over the 1st and 2nd, 5th and 6th sc + 1 tch (4)

ROW 30: turn around and dec over the 1st and 2nd, 3rd and 4th sc (2)

Tie-off.

Now you need to go back to row 28 again.

ROW 28: attach yarn to the other side of row 28 and crochet 6 sc + 1 tch (6)

ROW 29: turn around and dec over the 1st and 2nd, 5th and 6th sc + 1 tch (4)

ROW 30: turn around and dec over the 1st and 2nd, 3rd and 4th sc (2)

Crochet an edge of sc around the belly and face. Crochet 2 sc in the stitches at row 30 to make them sharper.

Tie-off with a sl.st and leave enough yarn for sewing.

BELLY/FACE

ARMS (2x)

(Use dark teal yarn)

RND 1: 6 sc in magic ring (6)

RND 2: 2 sc in each sc (12)

RND 3: 2 sc in each 4th sc (15)

RND 4: 15 sc (15)

RND 5: 2 sc in each 5th sc (18)

RND 6–11: 18 sc (18)

Fill the arms. Tie-off with a sl.st and leave enough yarn for sewing.

FINGERNAILS (10x)

(Use light blue yarn)

ROW 1: 1 ch + 1 tch (1)

ROW 2: turn around and crochet 1 sl.st (1)

Tie-off and leave enough yarn for sewing.

TOENAILS (6x)

(Use light blue yarn)

ROW 1: 2 ch + 1 tch (2)

ROW 2: turn around and crochet 1 sl.st, 1 sc (2)

Tie-off and leave enough yarn for sewing.

ARM

FINGERNAILS ASSEMBLY

TOENAILS ASSEMBLY

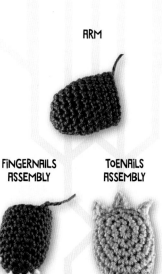

EARS (2x)

(Use dark teal yarn)

RND 1: 6 sc in magic ring (6)

RND 2: 6 sc (6)

RND 3: 2 sc in each sc (12)

RND 4: 12 sc (12)

RND 5: 2 sc in each 2nd sc (18)

RND 6: 18 sc (18)

Fill the ears. Tie-off with a sl.st and leave enough yarn for sewing.

FEET (2x)

(Use cream yarn)

RND 1: 6 sc in magic ring (6)

RND 2: 2 sc in each sc (12)

RND 3: 2 sc in the 1st, 2nd, 3rd, 7th, 8th, 9th sc (18)

RND 4: 2 sc in the 2nd, 4th, 6th, 11th, 13th, 15th sc (24)

RND 5: 2 sc in the 4th, 5th, 6th, 16th, 17th, 18th sc (30)

RND 6: 30 sc (30)

RND 7: dec over the 1st and 2nd, 3rd and 4th, 5th and 6th, 7th and 8th, 9th and 10th, 11th and 12th sc (24)

RND 8: dec over each 3rd and 4th sc (18)

Fill the feet. Tie-off with a sl.st and leave enough yarn for sewing.

ASSEMBLY

Sew the face and belly to the head and body, at round 7 to round 35.

Sew the arms to the body, at round 18 to round 23.

Sew five fingernails to each arm.

Sew the feet to the bottom of the body, at round 39 to round 45.

Sew three toenails to each foot, between rounds 4 and 5.

Cut two paw pads out of brown felt and glue them to the bottom of the feet.

Sew the ears to the head, at round 5 to round 9.

FACE

Embroider two eyes with thin black yarn to the face, between rows 26 and 27, with four stitches between the eyes.

Embroider a mouth to the face with thin black yarn, at round 23.

Cut two teeth out of white felt. Glue them to the face, above the mouth.

FOOT

EAR

EEVEE

OFFICIAL COLORS

NATIONAL POKÉDEX NO.	TYPE	WEIGHT	HEIGHT
133	Normal	14.3 lb / 6.5 kg	1 ft / 0.3 m

Because it can evolve into so many different Pokémon, researchers believe that Eevee's genes could help them figure out exactly how Pokémon Evolution works.

MATERIALS

- Crochet hook 2.5 mm
- 60 grams light brown yarn (I used SMC Catania—179)
- 25 grams off-white acrylic yarn (I used Stylecraft Special 4 ply—1005)
- 5 grams dark brown yarn (I used Phildar Phil Coton 3—Havane 1388)
- Fiberfill
- Black, white, and pink felt
- Thin black yarn (I used Durable Embroidery-crochet cotton—1001)
- Brush

Finished size approximately
6¼ inches (16 cm) high

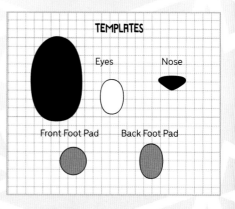

TEMPLATES

Eyes

Nose

Front Foot Pad   Back Foot Pad

HEAD

(Use light brown yarn)

RND 1: 6 sc in magic ring (6)

RND 2: 2 sc in each sc (12)

RND 3: 2 sc in each 2nd sc (18)

RND 4: 2 sc in each 3rd sc (24)

RND 5: 2 sc in each 4th sc (30)

RND 6: 2 sc in each 5th sc (36)

RND 7: 2 sc in each 6th sc (42)

RND 8: 2 sc in each 14th sc (45)

RND 9–14: 45 sc (45)

RND 15: 2 sc in the 18th, 21st, 24th, 27th sc (49)

RND 16: 2 sc in the 19th, 23rd, 27th, 31st sc (53)

RND 17–19: 53 sc (53)

RND 20: dec over the 19th and 20th, 24th and 25th, 29th and 30th, 34th and 35th sc (49)

RND 21: dec over the 18th and 19th, 22nd and 23rd, 26th and 27th, 30th and 31st sc (45)

RND 22: dec over each 14th and 15th sc (42)

RND 23: dec over each 6th and 7th sc (36)

RND 24: dec over each 5th and 6th sc (30)

RND 25: dec over each 4th and 5th sc (24)

RND 26: dec over each 3rd and 4th sc (18)

Fill the head. Tie-off with a sl.st and leave enough yarn for sewing.

BODY

(Use light brown yarn)

RND 1: 6 sc in magic ring (6)

RND 2: 2 sc in each sc (12)

RND 3: 2 sc in each 2nd sc (18)

RND 4: 2 sc in each 3rd sc (24)

RND 5: 2 sc in each 4th sc (30)

RND 6: 2 sc in each 5th sc (36)

RND 7–24: 36 sc (36)

RND 25: dec over each 5th and 6th sc (30)

RND 26: dec over each 4th and 5th sc (24)

RND 27: dec over each 3rd and 4th sc (18)

Fill the body and keep filling until the last round.

RND 28: dec over each 2nd and 3rd sc (12)

RND 29: dec over each 2 sc (6)

Tie-off with a sl.st and close the body.

HEAD

BODY

FORELEGS (2X)

(Use light brown yarn)

RND 1: 6 sc in magic ring (6)

RND 2: 2 sc in each sc (12)

RND 3: 2 sc in the 1st, 2nd, 3rd, 4th sc (16)

RND 4: 16 sc (16)

RND 5: dec over the 1st and 2nd, 3rd and 4th, 5th and 6th, 7th and 8th sc (12)

RND 6–9: 12 sc (12)

RND 10: 2 sc in each 4th sc (15)

RND 11: 15 sc (15)

Fill the legs. Tie-off with a sl.st and leave enough yarn for sewing.

HIND LEGS (2X)

(Use light brown yarn)

RND 1: 6 sc in magic ring (6)

RND 2: 2 sc in each sc (12)

RND 3: 2 sc in the 1st, 2nd, 3rd, 4th sc (16)

RND 4: dec over the 1st and 2nd, 3rd and 4th, 5th and 6th, 7th and 8th sc, 2 sc in the 11th, 12th, 13th, 14th sc (16)

RND 5: dec over the 1st and 2nd, 3rd and 4th, 5th and 6th, 15th and 16th sc (12)

RND 6–9: 12 sc (12)

RND 10: 2 sc in each 2nd sc (18)

RND 11–12: 18 sc (18)

Fill the legs. Tie-off with a sl.st and leave enough yarn for sewing.

TAIL

(Start with off-white acrylic yarn)

RND 1: 6 sc in magic ring (6)

RND 2: 6 sc (6)

RND 3: 2 sc in each sc (12)

RND 4–5: 12 sc (12)

RND 6: 2 sc in each 2nd sc (18)

RND 7–8: 18 sc (18)

RND 9: 2 sc in each 3rd sc (24)

RND 10: 24 sc (24)

RND 11: 2 sc in each 4th sc (30)

RND 12: 30 sc (30)

RND 13: 2 sc in each 5th sc (36)

(Switch to light brown yarn)

RND 14: 36 sc (36)

RND 15: 2 sc in each 6th sc (42)

RND 16–26: 42 sc (42)

RND 27: dec over each 6th and 7th sc (36)

RND 28: 36 sc (36)

RND 29: dec over each 5th and 6th sc (30)

RND 30: 30 sc (30)

RND 31: dec over each 4th and 5th sc (24)

RND 32: dec over each 3rd and 4th sc (18)

Fill the tail. Tie-off with a sl.st and leave enough yarn for sewing. Brush the end of the tail out to make it fluffy.

FORELEG

HIND LEG

TAIL

OUTER EARS (2x)

(Use light brown yarn)

RND 1: 4 sc in magic ring (4)

RND 2: 4 sc (4)

RND 3: 2 sc in each sc (8)

RND 4: 8 sc (8)

RND 5: 2 sc in each 4th sc (10)

RND 6: 10 sc (10)

RND 7: 2 sc in each 5th sc (12)

RND 8: 12 sc (12)

RND 9: 2 sc in each 4th sc (15)

RND 10–11: 15 sc (15)

RND 12: 2 sc in each 5th sc (18)

RND 13–15: 18 sc (18)

RND 16: dec over each 5th and 6th sc (15)

RND 17–18: 15 sc (15)

RND 19: dec over each 4th and 5th sc (12)

RND 20: 12 sc (12)

Tie-off with a sl.st and leave enough yarn for sewing.

INNER EARS (2x)

(Use dark brown yarn)

ROW 1: 14 ch + 1 tch (14)

ROW 2: turn around and crochet 1 sl.st, 2 sc, 8 hdc, 2 sc, 1 sl.st, continue on the other side of the chain, crochet 1 sl.st, 2 sc, 8 hdc, 2 sc, 1 sl.st

Tie-off and leave enough yarn for sewing.

OUTER EAR   **INNER EAR**

a1

a2

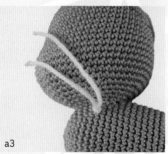

a3

a4

ASSEMBLY

Sew the head to the body, at round 6 to round 12.

Sew the legs to the body. Sew the forelegs at round 6 to round 10, and the hind legs at round 18 to round 23.

To create the toes, make two stitch lines with light brown yarn on the front of the feet, and pull them tight.

Cut four paw pads out of pink felt. Glue them to the bottom of the legs.

Sew the tail to the back of the body.

Sew the inner ears to the outer ears. Then sew the ears to the head, at round 7 to round 11.

COLLAR

Attach pieces of off-white acrylic yarn to the body (images a1–a4).

Make about four rows around the body below the head.

Brush the yarn out to make it fluffy.

FACE

Cut two eyes out of black and white felt. Glue them onto the head, at round 10 to round 16, with six stitches between the eyes.

Cut a nose out of black felt. Glue it onto the head, at round 16.

Embroider a mouth to the head with thin black yarn, at round 18.

Embroider two eyebrows to the head with thin black yarn, at round 9.

PiKACHU

OFFICIAL COLORS

NATIONAL POKÉDEX No.	TYPE	WEIGHT	HEIGHT
25	Electric	13.2 lb / 6.0 kg	1ft 4 in / 0.4 m

If you come across a Pikachu in its forest home, watch out for its red cheeks! That's where it stores electricity, so if you touch them, you'll get zapped.

MATERIALS

- Crochet hook 2.5 mm

- 70 grams of yellow yarn (I used Yarn and Colors Must-Have—013)

- 5 grams of black yarn (I used Phildar Phil Coton 3—Noir 1200)

- 10 grams of brown yarn (I used Phildar Phil Coton 3—Havane 1388)

- Fiberfill

- Black, white, and red felt

- Thin black yarn (I used Rico Essentials Crochet—12)

Finished size approximately 6¹/₂ inches (17 cm) high

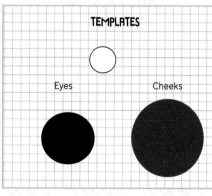

TEMPLATES

Eyes

Cheeks

HEAD/BODY

(Use yellow yarn)

RND 1: 6 sc in magic ring (6)

RND 2: 2 sc in each sc (12)

RND 3: 2 sc in each 2nd sc (18)

RND 4: 2 sc in each 3rd sc (24)

RND 5: 2 sc in each 4th sc (30)

RND 6: 2 sc in each 5th sc (36)

RND 7: 2 sc in each 6th sc (42)

RND 8: 2 sc in each 7th sc (48)

RND 9: 2 sc in each 8th sc (54)

RND 10–17: 54 sc (54)

RND 18: 2 sc in the 6th, 10th, 14th, 18th, 22nd, 26th sc (60)

RND 19–21: 60 sc (60)

RND 22: dec over the 6th and 7th, 11th and 12th, 16th and 17th, 21st and 22nd, 26th and 27th, 31st and 32nd sc (54)

RND 23: dec over each 8th and 9th sc (48)

RND 24: dec over each 7th and 8th sc (42)

RND 25: 2 sc in each 7th sc (48)

RND 26: 48 sc (48)

RND 27: 2 sc in the 3rd, 9th, 27th, 33rd, 39th, 45th sc (54)

RND 28: 54 sc (54)

RND 29: 2 sc in each 9th sc (60)

RND 30: 60 sc (60)

RND 31: 2 sc in the 3rd, 10th, 35th, 42nd, 49th, 56th sc (66)

RND 32–40: 66 sc (66)

RND 41: dec over the 4th and 5th, 12th and 13th, 15th and 16th, 18th and 19th, 21st and 22nd, 30th and 31st, 33rd and 34th, 36th and 37th, 38th and 39th, 46th and 47th, 54th and 55th, 62nd and 63rd sc (54)

Start filling and keep filling until the last round.

RND 42: dec over each 8th and 9th sc (48)

RND 43: dec over each 7th and 8th sc (42)

RND 44: dec over each 6th and 7th sc (36)

RND 45: dec over each 5th and 6th sc (30)

RND 46: dec over each 4th and 5th sc (24)

RND 47: dec over each 3rd and 4th sc (18)

RND 48: dec over each 2nd and 3rd sc (12)

RND 49: dec over each 2 sc (6)

Tie-off with a sl.st and close the body.

EARS (2X)

(Start with black yarn)

RND 1: 6 sc in magic ring (6)

RND 2: 6 sc (6)

RND 3: 2 sc in each 2nd sc (9)

RND 4: 9 sc (9)

RND 5: 2 sc in each 3rd sc (12)

RND 6: 2 sc in each 4th sc (15)

(In the next rounds you switch between yellow and black yarn)

RND 7: 3 sc in yellow, 10 sc in black, 2 sc in yellow (15)

RND 8: 5 sc in yellow, 6 sc in black, 4 sc in yellow (15)

RND 9: 7 sc in yellow, 2 sc in black, 6 sc in yellow (15)

(Continue with yellow yarn)

RND 10–18: 15 sc (15)

RND 19: dec over each 4th and 5th sc (12)

RND 20: 12 sc (12)

Fill the ears. Tie-off with a sl.st and leave enough yarn for sewing.

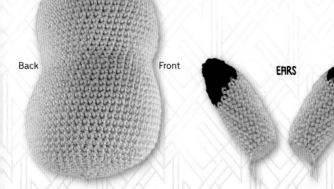

HEAD/BODY

Back   Front   **EARS**

FEET (2x)

(Use yellow yarn)

RND 1: 6 sc in magic ring (6)

RND 2: 2 sc in each 2nd sc (9)

RND 3: 9 sc (9)

RND 4: 2 sc in each 3rd sc (12)

RND 5: 12 sc (12)

RND 6: 2 sc in each 4th sc (15)

RND 7–9: 15 sc (15)

RND 10: dec over each 4th and 5th sc (12)

RND 11: dec over each 2 sc (6)

Tie-off with a sl.st and close the feet. Let the yarn come out on the top of the feet and leave enough for sewing.

ARMS (2x)

(Use yellow yarn)

RND 1: 6 sc in magic ring (6)

RND 2: 2 sc in each sc (12)

RND 3–4: 12 sc (12)

RND 5: 2 sc in each 4th sc (15)

RND 6–9: 15 sc (15)

RND 10: dec over each 4th and 5th sc (12)

RND 11: 12 sc (12)

RND 12: dec over each 3rd and 4th sc (9)

RND 13: 9 sc (9)

RND 14: dec over each 2nd and 3rd sc (6)

Tie-off with a sl.st and close the arms. Let the yarn come out on the side of the arms and leave enough for sewing.

STRiPES (2x)

(Use brown yarn)

ROW 1: 16 ch + 1 tch (16)

ROW 2: turn around and crochet 16 sc (16)

Tie-off with a sl.st and leave enough yarn for sewing.

TAIL (2x)

(Start with yellow yarn)

ROW 1: 15 ch + 1 tch (15)

ROW 2: turn around and crochet 15 sc + 1 tch (15)

ROW 3: turn around and dec over the 14th and 15th sc + 1 tch (14)

ROW 4: turn around and crochet 14 sc + 1 tch (14)

ROW 5: turn around and dec over the 13th and 14th sc + 1 tch (13)

ROW 6: turn around and crochet 13 sc + 1 tch (13)

ROW 7: turn around and dec over the 12th and 13th sc + 1 tch (12)

ROW 8: turn around and crochet 12 sc + 1 tch (12)

ROW 9: turn around and crochet 5 sc (don't crochet in the other 7 sc) + 1 tch (5)

ROW 10–11: turn around and crochet 5 sc + 1 tch (5)

ROW 12: turn around and crochet 5 sc and 4 ch + 1 tch (9)

ROW 13–16: turn around and crochet 9 sc + 1 tch (9)

a1

a2

FEET   ARM   STRiPE   TAIL

ROW 17: turn around and crochet 4 sc (don't crochet in the other 5 sc) + 1 tch (4)

(In the next round you switch between yellow and brown yarn)

ROW 18: 1 sc in yellow, 1 sc in brown, 1 sc in yellow, 1 sc in brown (4)

(Continue with brown yarn)

ROW 19: turn around and crochet 4 sc + 1 tch (4)

ROW 20: turn around and crochet 4 sc and 3 ch + 1 tch (7)

ROW 21: turn around and crochet 7 sc + 1 tch (7)

ROW 22: turn around and crochet 7 sc (7)

Tie-off (image a1).

Put the two tails on top of each other. Crochet them together with an edge of sc. Crochet 3 sc in the stitches at the corners for more sharpness (image a2).

Leave enough yarn for sewing.

ASSEMBLY

Sew the ears to the head, at round 8 to round 11.

Sew the arms at right angles to the body, starting at round 27.

To create the fingers, make two stitch lines with yellow yarn on the end of the arms and pull them tight.

Sew the feet to the bottom of the body. To create the toes, make two stitch lines with yellow yarn on the front of the feet, and pull them tight.

Sew the stripes to the back. Sew the first stripe at round 29 and the second stripe about round 34.

Sew the tail to the body at round 40. To keep the tail up, attach it at another higher point on the body as well.

FACE

Cut two eyes out of black and white felt. Glue them onto the head, at round 12 to round 16, with seven stitches between the eyes.

Sew a cute little nose with thin black yarn, at round 16.

Split a piece of the black yarn to make it thinner and use it to sew a mouth to the head, at round 19.

Cut two cheeks out of red felt. Glue these onto the head, at round 17 to round 22.

PSYDUCK

OFFICIAL COLORS

NATIONAL POKÉDEX NO.	TYPE	WEIGHT	HEIGHT
54	Water	43.2 lb / 19.6 kg	2 ft 7 in / 0.8 m

Poor Psyduck suffers from relentless headaches. No one knows for certain if the psychic powers it uses are intentional, or if they just get out of control sometimes.

MATERIALS

- Crochet hook 2.5 mm
- 60 grams of yellow yarn (I used Scheepjes Catona—208)
- 20 grams of cream yarn (I used Scheepjes Catona—404)
- 5 grams of black yarn (I used Phildar Phil Coton 3—Noir 1200)
- Fiberfill
- White felt
- Black textile marker
- Thin black yarn (for instance Rico Essentials Crochet - 12)

Finished size approximately 5 inches (13 cm) high

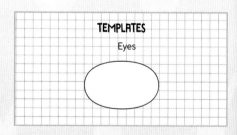

TEMPLATES

Eyes

HEAD/BODY

(Use yellow yarn)

RND 1: 6 sc in magic ring (6)

RND 2: 2 sc in each sc (12)

RND 3: 2 sc in each 2nd sc (18)

RND 4: 2 sc in each 3rd sc (24)

RND 5: 2 sc in each 4th sc (30)

RND 6: 2 sc in each 5th sc (36)

RND 7: 2 sc in each 6th sc (42)

RND 8: 2 sc in each 7th sc (48)

RND 9: 2 sc in each 16th sc (51)

RND 10–15: 51 sc (51)

RND 16: dec over each 16th and 17th sc (48)

RND 17: dec over each 7th and 8th sc (42)

RND 18: dec over each 6th and 7th sc (36)

RND 19: dec over each 5th and 6th sc (30)

RND 20: 2 sc in each 5th sc (36)

RND 21: 2 sc in each 6th sc (42)

RND 22: 2 sc in each 7th sc (48)

RND 23: 2 sc in each 8th sc (54)

RND 24: 2 sc in each 9th sc (60)

RND 25–35: 60 sc (60)

RND 36: dec over each 9th and 10th sc (54)

RND 37: dec over each 8th and 9th sc (48)

RND 38: dec over each 7th and 8th sc (42)

RND 39: dec over each 6th and 7th sc (36)

RND 40: dec over each 5th and 6th sc (30)

RND 41: dec over each 4th and 5th sc (24)

Start filling and keep filling until the last round.

RND 42: dec over each 3rd and 4th sc (18)

RND 43: dec over each 2nd and 3rd sc (12)

RND 44: dec over each 2 sc (6)

Tie-off with a sl.st and close the head/body.

TOES (6X)

(Use cream yarn)

RND 1: 4 sc in magic ring (4)

RND 2: 4 sc (4)

Tie-off four toes with a sl.st. Do not tie-off the other two toes. Continue with the feet.

FEET (2X)

(Use cream yarn)

In the next round you will join three toes to create the foot.

RND 3: lay three toes next to each other with the toe that you didn't tie-off on the right.

Step 1. go to the middle toe and crochet 2 sc (image a1),

Step 2. go to the left toe and crochet 4 sc (image a2),

Step 3. continue with the middle toe and crochet 2 sc,

Step 4. go to the right toe and crochet 4 sc (12).

RND 4: dec over each 3rd and 4th sc (9)

RND 5–6: 9 sc (9)

RND 7: dec over each 2nd and 3rd sc (6)

Tie-off with a sl.st and close the feet. Let the yarn come out on the top of the feet and leave enough for sewing (image a3).

HEAD/BODY

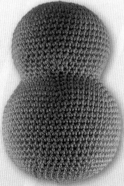

TOES

a1

a2

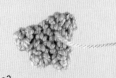

a3

ARMS (2x)

(Use yellow yarn)

RND 1: 6 sc in magic ring (6)

RND 2: 2 sc in each sc (12)

RND 3: 2 sc in each 4th sc (15)

RND 4–8: 15 sc (15)

RND 9: dec over each 4th and 5th sc (12)

RND 10–11: 12 sc (12)

Fill the arms. You don't need to fill the next rounds.

RND 12: dec over each 3rd and 4th sc (9)

RND 13: 9 sc (9)

RND 14: crochet 3 sc and finish with a sl.st in the 1st sc (images a1, a2),

Step 1. attach yarn to the 3rd sc (image a3) and crochet 1 sc in the 4th, 5th and 9th sc, finish with a sl.st in the 4th sc (image a4),

Step 2. attach yarn to the 5th sc and crochet 1 sc in the 6th, 7th and 8th sc, finish with a sl.st in the 6th sc (images a5, a6).

Let some yarn come out on the bottom of the arm and leave enough for sewing.

a1

a2

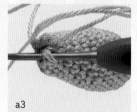

a3

a4

a5

a6

TAIL

(Use yellow yarn)

RND 1: 6 sc in magic ring (6)

RND 2: 6 sc (6)

RND 3: 2 sc in each 2nd sc (9)

RND 4: 9 sc (9)

RND 5: 2 sc in each 3rd sc (12)

RND 6: 12 sc (12)

RND 7: 2 sc in each 4th sc (15)

RND 8: 15 sc (15)

RND 9: 4 sc, 2 hdc, 3 dc, 2 hdc, 4 sc (15)

Fill the tail. Tie-off with a sl.st and leave enough yarn for sewing.

TAIL   ARM

HAIR

(Use black yarn)

5 ch + 1 tch, turn around and crochet 5 sl.st,

5 ch + 1 tch, turn around and crochet 5 sl.st,

5 ch + 1 tch, turn around and crochet 5 sl.st

Tie-off and leave enough yarn for sewing.

BEAK

(Use cream yarn)

RND 1: 9 ch + 1 tch (9)

RND 2: turn around and crochet 9 sc, continue on the other side of the row and crochet 9 sc (18)

Don't turn around, but continue crocheting in rounds.

RND 3: 2 sc in the 1st, 9th, 10th, 18th sc (22)

RND 4: 2 sc in the 1st, 2nd, 10th, 11th, 12th, 13th, 21st, 22nd sc (30)

RND 5–11: 30 sc (30)

RND 12: dec over each 4th and 5th sc (24)

RND 13–15: 24 sc (24)

RND 16: 2 sc in each 4th sc (30)

RND 17: 2 sc in the 5th, 6th, 12th, 13th, 14th, 20th, 21st sc (37)

Fill the beak slightly. Tie-off with a sl.st and leave enough yarn for sewing.

ASSEMBLY

Sew the feet to the bottom of the body.

Sew the arms to the head and body, at round 10 to round 25.

Sew the tail to the body, at round 31 to round 35.

Sew the beak to the head, at round 12 to round 19.

Sew the hair to the top of the head.

FACE

Cut two eyes out of white felt. Glue them onto the head, at round 9 to round 12, with five stitches between the eyes.

Use a black textile marker to make the pupils.

Embroider two nostrils to the beak with thin black yarn, at round 16.

HAIR

BEAK

VULPIX

OFFICIAL COLORS

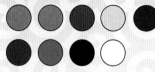

NATIONAL POKÉDEX NO.	TYPE	WEIGHT	HEIGHT
37	Fire	21.8 lb / 9.9 kg	2 ft / 0.6 m

Vulpix has lovely fur and many elegant tails. As this Fire-type Pokémon gets older, the number of tails increases, as its existing tails split and grow.

MATERIALS

- Crochet hook 2.5 mm

- 60 grams of orange-brown yarn (I used Yarn and Colors Must-Have—Bronze 018)

- 50 gram of red-brown yarn (I used Yarn and Colors Must-Have—Brick 023)

- 10 grams of off-white yarn (I used Phildar Phil Coton 3—Craie 1397)

- 5 grams of dark brown yarn (I used Phildar Phil Coton 3—Havane 1388)

- Fiberfill

- Brown, dark brown, light brown, white, and black felt

Finished size approximately 6¹/₄ inches (16 cm) high

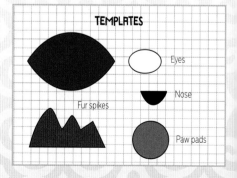

TEMPLATES

Eyes

Nose

Fur spikes

Paw pads

HEAD

(Use orange-brown yarn)

RND 1: 6 sc in magic ring (6)

RND 2: 2 sc in each sc (12)

RND 3: 2 sc in each 2nd sc (18)

RND 4: 18 sc (18)

RND 5: 2 sc in each 3rd sc (24)

RND 6: 24 sc (24)

RND 7: 2 sc in each 4th sc (30)

RND 8: 30 sc (30)

RND 9: 2 sc in each 5th sc (36)

RND 10: 36 sc (36)

RND 11: 2 sc in each 6th sc (42)

RND 12: 2 sc in each 7th sc (48)

RND 13: 2 sc in each 8th sc (54)

RND 14–20: 54 sc (54)

RND 21: dec over each 8th and 9th sc (48)

RND 22: 48 sc (48)

RND 23: dec over each 7th and 8th sc (42)

RND 24: 42 sc (42)

RND 25: dec over each 6th and 7th sc (36)

RND 26: dec over each 5th and 6th sc (30)

RND 27: dec over each 4th and 5th sc (24)

Start filling and keep filling until the last round.

RND 28: dec over each 3rd and 4th sc (18)

RND 29: dec over each 2nd and 3rd sc (12)

RND 30: dec over each 2 sc (6)

Tie-off with a sl.st and close the head.

NECK

(Use orange-brown yarn)

Leave enough yarn at the beginning for sewing.

RND 1: 30 ch and finish with a sl.st in the 1st ch to connect the chain (30)

RND 2: 30 sc (30)

Tie-off with a sl.st and leave enough yarn for sewing.

BODY

(Use orange-brown yarn)

RND 1: 6 sc in magic ring (6)

RND 2: 2 sc in each sc (12)

RND 3: 2 sc in each 2nd sc (18)

RND 4: 2 sc in each 3rd sc (24)

RND 5: 2 sc in each 4th sc (30)

RND 6: 2 sc in each 5th sc (36)

RND 7: 2 sc in each 12th sc (39)

RND 8–24: 39 sc (39)

RND 25: dec over each 12th and 13th sc (36)

RND 26: dec over each 5th and 6th sc (30)

RND 27: dec over each 4th and 5th sc (24)

Start filling and keep filling until the last round.

RND 28: dec over each 3rd and 4th sc (18)

RND 29: dec over each 2nd and 3rd sc (12)

RND 30: dec over each 2 sc (6)

Tie-off with a sl.st and close the body.

NECK

HEAD

BODY

TAILS (6x)

(Use red-brown yarn)

RND 1: 6 sc in magic ring (6)

RND 2: 2 sc in each sc (12)

RND 3–23: 12 sc, fill the tails regularly (12)

RND 24: dec over each 3rd and 4th sc (9)

RND 25–26: 9 sc (9)

RND 27: dec over each 2nd and 3rd sc (6)

Tie-off five tails with a sl.st. Don't tie-off tail six just yet.

a1

Joining the tails

In the next round you will join the six tails to make one part.

RND 28: continue with tail six; lay the six tails next to each other:

Step 1. go to tail one and crochet 3 sc (image a1),

Step 2. go to tail two and crochet 3 sc (image a2),

Step 3. go to tail three and crochet 3 sc,

Step 4. go to tail four and crochet 3 sc,

Step 5. go to tail five and crochet 6 sc,

Step 6. continue with tail four and crochet 3 sc,

Step 7. continue with tail three and crochet 3 sc,

Step 8. continue with tail two and crochet 3 sc,

Step 9. continue with tail one and crochet 3 sc,

Step 10. go to tail six and crochet 6 sc (36)

Tie-off with a sl.st and leave enough yarn for sewing.

Roll the ends of the tails. Use (fabric) glue to keep them in the rolled position.

a2

TAIL

b1

HEAD CURLS (3x)

(Use red-brown yarn)

RND 1: 5 sc in magic ring (5)

RND 2: 2 sc in each sc (10)

RND 3–19: 10 sc, fill the curls regularly (10)

Tie-off two curls with a sl.st. Don't tie-off curl three yet.

Joining the curls

In the next round you will join the three curls together to make one piece.

RND 20: continue with curl three, lay the three curls next to each other (image b1),

Step 1. go to curl one and crochet 5 sc (image b2),

Step 2. go to curl two and crochet 10 sc (image b3),

Step 3. return to curl one and crochet the other 5 sc,

Step 4. go to curl three and crochet 10 sc (30) (image b4)

Tie-off with a sl.st and leave enough yarn for sewing. Roll the ends of the curls. Use (fabric) glue to keep them rolled up.

b2

b3

b4

FRONT HAIR

PART 1

(Use red-brown yarn)

RND 1: 5 sc in magic ring (5)

RND 2: 5 sc (5)

Tie-off with a sl.st.

PART 2

(Use red-brown yarn)

RND 1: 5 sc in magic ring (5)

RND 2: 5 sc (5)

Tie-off with a sl.st.

c1

PART 3

(Use red-brown yarn)

RND 1: 6 sc in magic ring (6)

RND 2: 6 sc (6)

RND 3: 2 sc in each 3rd sc (8)

RND 4: 8 sc (8)

RND 5: 2 sc in each 4th sc (10)

RND 6: 10 sc (10)

c2

RND 7: crochet around the three parts:

 Step 1. first crochet 5 sc of part one
 (image c1),

Step 2. go to part three and crochet 5 sc,

Step 3. then crochet 5 sc of part two
(image c2),

Step 4. continue with part three and crochet
the other 5 sc (20)

RND 8: 2 sc in each 4th sc (25)

RND 9: 25 sc (25)

RND 10: dec over each 4th and 5th sc (20)

Tie-off with a sl.st and leave enough yarn
for sewing (image c3).

FRONT HAIR

BACK HAIR

PART 1

(Use red-brown yarn)

RND 1: 5 sc in magic ring (5)

RND 2: 5 sc (5)

Tie-off with a sl.st.

PART 2

(Use red-brown yarn)

RND 1: 5 sc in magic ring (5)

RND 2: 5 sc (5)

Tie-off with a sl.st.

PART 3

(Use red-brown yarn)

RND 1: 5 sc in magic ring (5)

RND 2: 5 sc (5)

RND 3: 2 sc in each sc (10)

RND 4: 10 sc (10)

RND 5: crochet around the three parts:

Step 1. first crochet 5 sc of part one,

Step 2. go to part three and crochet 5 sc,

Step 3. then crochet 5 sc of part two,

Step 4. continue with part three and crochet the other 5 sc (20)

Tie-off with a sl.st and leave enough yarn for sewing.

FORELEGS (2x)

(Start with dark brown yarn)

RND 1: 6 sc in magic ring (6)

RND 2: 2 sc in the 1st, 2nd, 4th, 5th sc (10)

RND 3: 2 sc in the 2nd, 4th, 7th, 9th sc (14)

RND 4: 14 sc (14)

RND 5: dec over the 2nd and 3rd, 5th and 6th sc (12)

RND 6–7: 12 sc (12)

(Switch to orange-brown yarn)

RND 8–9: 12 sc (12)

RND 10: 2 sc in each 4th sc (15)

RND 11–12: 15 sc (15)

Fill the legs. Tie-off with a sl.st and leave enough yarn for sewing.

BELLY

(Use off-white yarn)

ROW 1: 4 ch + 1 tch (4)

ROW 2: turn around and crochet 2 sc in the 1st, 4th ch + 1 tch (6)

ROW 3–24: turn around and crochet 6 sc + 1 tch (6)

ROW 25: turn around and dec over the 1st and 2nd, 5th and 6th sc (4)

Crochet an edge of sc around the belly.

Tie-off with a sl.st and leave enough yarn for sewing.

BACK HAIR

FORELEG

BELLY

HIND LEGS (2x)

(Start with dark brown yarn)

RND 1: 6 sc in magic ring (6)

RND 2: 2 sc in the 1st, 2nd, 4th, 5th sc (10)

RND 3: 2 sc in the 2nd, 4th, 7th, 9th sc (14)

RND 4: 14 sc (14)

RND 5: dec over the 2nd and 3rd, 5th, and 6th sc (12)

RND 6: 12 sc (12)

(Switch to orange-brown yarn)

RND 7–8: 12 sc (12)

RND 9: 2 sc in each 2nd sc (18)

RND 10–12: 18 sc (18)

Fill the legs. Tie-off with a sl.st and leave enough yarn for sewing.

OUTER EARS (2x)

(Use orange-brown yarn)

RND 1: 6 sc in magic ring (6)

RND 2: 6 sc (6)

RND 3: 2 sc in each sc (12)

RND 4: 12 sc (12)

RND 5: 2 sc in each 2nd sc (18)

RND 6: 18 sc (18)

RND 7: 2 sc in each 3rd sc (24)

RND 8–11: 24 sc (24)

Tie-off with a sl.st and leave enough yarn for sewing.

INNER EARS (2x)

(Use dark brown yarn)

ROW 1: 1 ch + 1 tch (1)

ROW 2: turn around and crochet 2 sc in the ch + 1 tch (2)

ROW 3: turn around and crochet 2 sc in the 2nd sc + 1 tch (3)

ROW 4: turn around and crochet 2 sc in the 3rd sc + 1 tch (4)

ROW 5: turn around and crochet 2 sc in the 4th sc + 1 tch (5)

ROW 6: turn around and crochet 2 sc in the 5th sc + 1 tch (6)

ROW 7: turn around and crochet 6 sc (6)

Tie-off and leave enough yarn for sewing.

HIND LEG

OUTER EAR

INNER EAR

ASSEMBLY

Sew one side of the neck to the head, at round 13 to round 19.

Sew the other side of the neck to the body, at round 6 to round 14.

Sew the belly to the body, with the beginning 3 rounds above the magic ring and the end at round 25.

Sew the forelegs to the body and a part of the belly, at round 4 to round 11. Sew the hind legs at round 19 to round 25.

Cut four paw pads out of light brown felt. Glue them onto the bottom of the legs.

Sew the tails to the body, at rounds 25 to 26.

Sew the curls to the head, at round 21 to round 23.

Sew the hair to the head in front of the curls, and the other hair behind the curls.

Sew the inner ears to the outer ears.

Then sew the ears to the head, at round 19 to round 24.

Cut fur spikes out of brown felt. Glue these onto the inner ears.

FACE

Cut two eyes out of dark brown and white felt. Glue them onto the head, at round 8 to round 14 , with five stitches between the eyes.

Cut a nose out of black felt and glue it onto the head, at round 2.

MEET THE AUTHOR

My name is Sabrina Somers. I live in the lovely city of Amsterdam in the Netherlands, with my husband Mark, our son Sven, our daughter Milou and two cats named Timmie and Sheila.

My crochet journey started back in 2014 when my husband bought me an amigurumi book as a gift. (Amigurumi is the incredibly popular Japanese art of crocheting small stuffed toys.) Thanks to that book I learned the different crochet stitches and I was able to create my first plush. By the end of 2014 I had made lots of different characters from various crochet books, and I was so taken with the craft that I decided to create my own amigurumi. By now I have designed over a 150 patterns and I love it!

I have been a big Pokémon fan since I was nine years old, I have literally lived with these incredible characters for years.

Who can forget the first time they saw Pikachu? I know I can't! It was love at first sight. I remember watching the TV series and following the adventures of Ash and Pikachu, and playing the games, first on the Game Boy and then on the DS. I loved the characters but most of all I loved the Pokémon themselves with all their wonderful colors and weird shapes.